B.B. King Anthology

B.B. King Anthology

Amsco Publications
New York • London • Sydney

Front and back cover photography by Luciano Viti/Retna Ltd.
Page 2 photograph by Luciano Viti/Retna Ltd.
Page 6 photograph by David Redfern/Retna Ltd.
Guitar transcriptions by Hemme Luttjeboer and John McCrea
Introduction by Walter Lindley

Order No. AM 85572
US International Standard Book Number: 0.8256.1317.5
UK International Standard Book Number: 0.7119.2734.0

Exclusive Distributors:
Music Sales Corporation
257 Park Avenue South, New York, NY 10010 USA
Music Sales Limited
8/9 Frith Street, London W1V 5TZ England
Music Sales Pty. Limited
120 Rothschild Street, Rosebery, Sydney, NSW 2018, Australia

Printed in the United States of America by
Vicks Lithograph and Printing Corporation

CONTENTS

Introduction

When you think of blues guitar, one name comes to mind: B.B. King. He is arguably the most influential, and certainly the most visible blues guitarist in history. Players such as Eric Clapton, Carlos Santana, Keith Richard, Billy Gibbons, and Mike Bloomfield have all acknowledged their debts to B.B King. And B.B.'s playing today remains as fresh and alive as ever.

Riley King was born in Mississippi in 1925, and by the age of fifteen was already playing on street corners. He had discovered that he could make more money in tips in one day of playing music than he could for a whole week's work picking cotton. Soon he was doing singing commercials on Memphis radio station WDIA, and from that he moved on to getting his own show. It was at this time that he picked up the nickname 'B.B.', short for "Blues Boy." His popularity grew, and eventually he was signed to the RPM record label. His first hit, "Three O'Clock Blues," went to number one on the Rhythm and Blues charts and heralded the arrival of a superstar. B.B. continued touring and recording throughout the fifties, but it wasn't until the sixties that his name became familiar to white audiences. Guitar players started picking up on B.B's unique voice, especially after hearing landmark recordings such as 1964's *Live at the Regal*. In 1970, he won a Grammy award for his monumental hit "The Thrill Is Gone." To this day he continues to tour over 250 days a year, and to record with his band and with artists as diverse as Larry Carlton and U2. His numerous television and film appearances, along with countless awards, continue to affirm his stature as an all-time blues great.

B.B. King's Guitar Style

B.B. King's style may seem simple, yet upon analysis it discloses a sophisticated awareness of melody, harmony, and rhythm. He always hits the "right" notes, phrases like no one else, and has a vibrato that is universally recognized. B.B. approaches the guitar as another voice, not just as an instrument: He plays as if he were singing through it. When he has to take a breath, his guitar does as well. He asserts that his sound is not something that he learned, it's just the way that he expresses himself as a person and as a musician.

Stylistically, what separates B.B. King from his peers is his firm rooting in the jazz, as well as the blues, idiom. One of B.B.'s major influences was jazz guitarist Lonnie Johnson, who was one of the first guitarists to visualize the guitar as a single-line solo instrument. B.B. also listened extensively to Charlie Christian, Django Reinhardt, and to horn players such as Lester Young, Johnny Hodges, and Bobby Hackett. His blues influence comes primarily from T-Bone Walker. B.B. softened Walker's somewhat strident style, adding a vibrato that he developed while trying to copy the bottleneck slide sound of his cousin Bukka White. The rest is pure B.B.—a combination of elements that has produced one of the most distinct blues voices ever.

B.B. draws from a large palette of harmonic and melodic devices. He is primarily known as a single-line player, though he does play chords—specifically triads and double stops, which he uses to punctuate his solos. Check out his chord intro to "Please Love Me" and his comping during the saxophone solo in "You Upset Me Baby." Here are a few voicings that B.B. commonly uses.

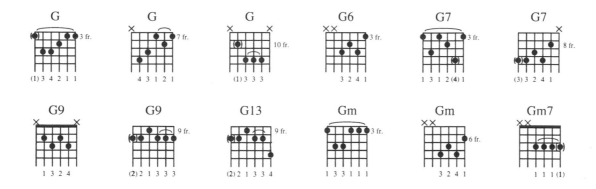

Perhaps the most identifiable feature of B.B.'s sound is his "bee-sting" vibrato. It comes completely from the wrist, as he shakes his whole hand rapidly and evenly. Even though this is a much-imitated sound, only B.B. can make it sing the way he does.

As most blues guitarists do, B.B. King primarily uses the minor pentatonic blues scale as a basis for his soloing ideas. Here are two of his favorite patterns.

What gives B.B. his unique slant on the blues, however, is his favorite scale pattern—a variation on the minor pentatonic scale that also includes a natural sixth and a natural ninth.

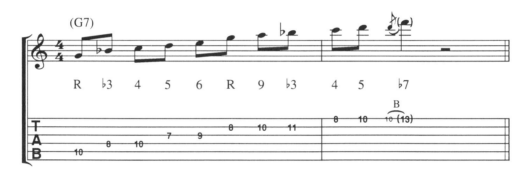

From this pattern, B.B. can bend the ninth to the flatted or natural third, the fifth to the sixth or flatted seventh, and the flatted seventh to the root. You can find examples of this pattern in both of the solos from "When Love Comes to Town."

Here is a variation on the previous pattern. In this one, B.B. plays a minor pentatonic scale with a natural sixth instead of a flatted seventh, then finishes it with a six-nine arpeggio.

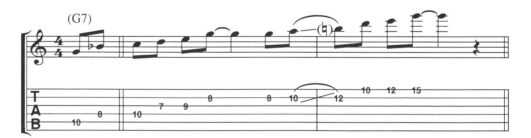

B.B.'s knowledge of jazz harmony allows him to introduce harmonic concepts into his soloing that are more sophisticated than the typical pentatonic ideas used by most blues guitarists. He plays off chord forms, often arpeggiating dominant ideas (such as the E♭7 run in measures 7 and 8 of the solo from "Please Love Me") or substituting other arpeggios over a dominant tonality (see measure 9 in the solo from "Sweet Little Angel" where he plays an E♭m9 arpeggio over an A♭7 chord, thus producing all of the tones found in an A♭13 chord). B.B. also uses chromaticism in his soloing (an obvious Charlie Christian influence). Check out measure 4 in the solo from "Please Love Me" to see how effective this approach can be.

The unique quality of B.B. King's style is his ability to combine jazzier elements with a rock-solid blues sensibility. As you play through the songs in this book, you'll find a wealth of information, emotion, and nuance which truly attest to B.B.'s title: "King of the Blues."

Legend of Musical Symbols

from Live At The Regal MCA 27006

Every Day I Have The Blues

by Peter Chapman

Fast shuffle

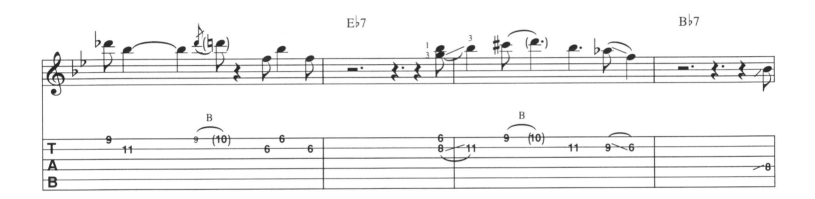

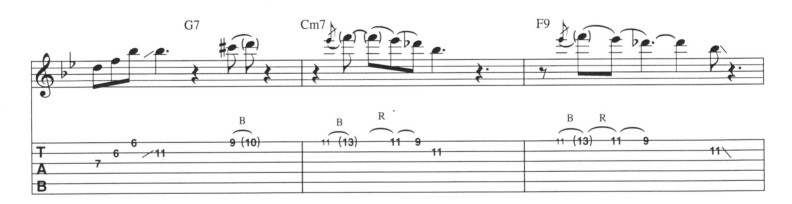

1. Ev - ery day,   Ev - ery day _

2., 3., 4. *See additional lyrics*

from The Best of B.B. King *MCA 27074*

The Thrill Is Gone

by B.B. King & Jules Taub

1. The thrill is gone, __
3., 5. See additional lyrics

The thrill is gone __ a- way, __

guitar 1 ad lib simile on repeats

guitar 2 simile on repeats

The thrill is gone, _ ba- by, The thrill is gone ___ a - way. _

You know you done me wrong, _ ba - by, And you'll be sor - ry some- day. _____

let ring -

let ring - - - - - -

2. The thrill is gone, _   It's gone a - way _ from me,
4.,6. See additional lyrics

guitar 1

P.M.

guitar 2 continues simile

hold bend

Em7

The thrill is gone, __ ba - by,   The thrill is gone a - way __ from me. __

Gmaj7   **F#7**   **Bm**   *to Coda*

Al - though I'll ___ still live on, _____   But so __ lone - ly __ I'll _____

Guitar solos 1 and 2

Bm

be. _____

rake

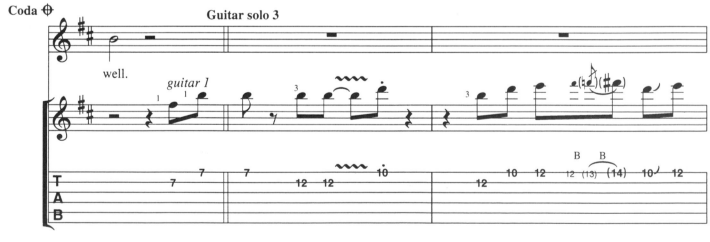

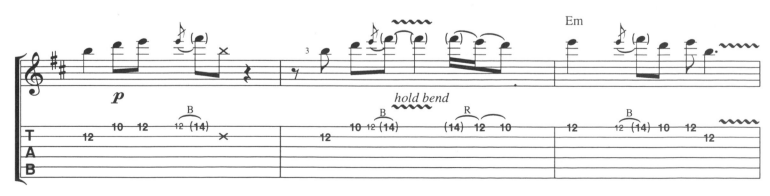

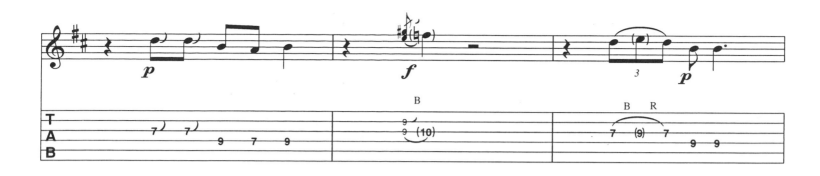

Additional lyrics

3. The thrill is gone,
   It's gone away for good,
   Oh, the thrill is gone,
   Baby, it's gone away for good.
   Someday I know I'll be over it all, baby,
   Just like I know a good man should.

4. You know I'm free, free now, baby,
   I'm free from your spell,
   Oh I'm free, free, free now,
   I'm free from your spell.
   And now that it's all over,
   All I can do is wish you well.

5. The thrill is gone,
   It's gone away for good,
   Oh, the thrill is gone,
   Baby, it's gone away for good.
   Someday I know I'll be over it all, baby,
   Just like I know a good man should.

6. You know I'm free, free now, baby,
   I'm free from your spell,
   Oh I'm free, free, free now,
   I'm free from your spell.
   And now that it's all over,
   All I can do is wish you well.

from U2: Rattle & Hum Island 422-842299

When Love Comes To Town

Words by Bono
Music by U2

24

did what I did ___ be - fore love _____ came to town.

with echo repeats

end Rhythm figure 1

guitar 2 (B.B. King)

(Bono:) 2. Used to make love __ un - der a red sun - set, __ Was mak - ing prom - is - es, I was

guitar 1

did what I did, _____ be - fore love _____ came to town.

with echo repeats

Guitar solo 2 (B.B. King)

(Bono:) Hey! _____ Yeah! _____

Additional lyrics

4. I was there when they crucified my Lord,
   I held the scabbard when the soldier drew his sword.
   I threw the dice when they pierced his side,
   But I've seen love conquer the Great Divide.

from Live At The Regal MCA 27006

Sweet Little Angel

by B.B. King & Jules Taub

(Spoken:) *"Thank you, I hope you remember that one."*

Additional lyrics

2. You know, I asked my baby for a nickel,
   And she gave me a twenty-dollar bill,
   Oh yes, I asked my baby for a nickel,
   And she gave me a twenty-dollar bill.
   Well, you know, I asked her for a little drink of liquor,
   And she gave me a whiskey still.

3. Oh yeah, if my baby was to quit me,
   Well, I do believe I would die,
   Oh yeah, if my baby was to quit me,
   Well, I do believe I would die.
   Yes, if you don't love me, little angel,
   Please tell me the reason why.

from The Electric B.B. King MCA 27007

Paying The Cost To Be The Boss

Words and Music by B.B. King

36

And play a lit-tle pok-er, too,   Don't you say noth-in' to me,

As long _ as I'm tak-in' care of you.   As long _ as I'm work-in', ba - by,

And pay-in' all the all   bills, want no   from you,

with Rhythm figure 1   E6   E9

A - bout _ the way I'm sup-posed to live. _____ You must be

E6   E9   B6   B9

cra - zy, wom - an,   Just got - ta be _____ out - ta your

B6   B9   F#6   F#9

mind. _____   As long - as I'm foot-in' the bills,

E6   E9   B6   B9   to Coda

I'm pay - in' the cost _____ of be- in' the

41

Coda

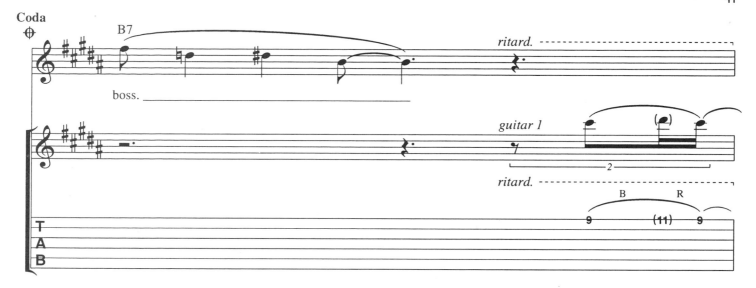

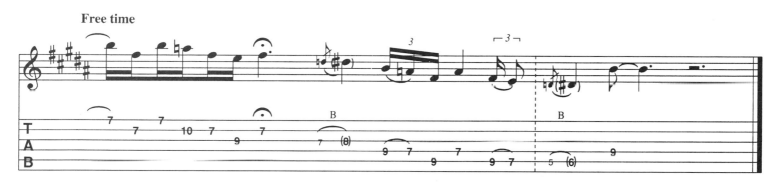

Additional lyrics

3. Now that you got me,
   You act like you're ashamed,
   You don't act like my woman,
   You're just usin' my name.
   I'll tell you I'm gonna handle all the money,
   And I don't want no back talk,
   'Cause if you don't like the way I'm doin',
   Just pick up your things and walk.

   You gotta be crazy, baby,
   Oh, you must be out of your mind.
   As long as I'm payin' the bills,
   I'm payin' the cost to be boss.

from Live "Now Appearing" At Ole Miss *MCA 8016*

Three O'Clock Blues

by B.B. King & Jules Taub

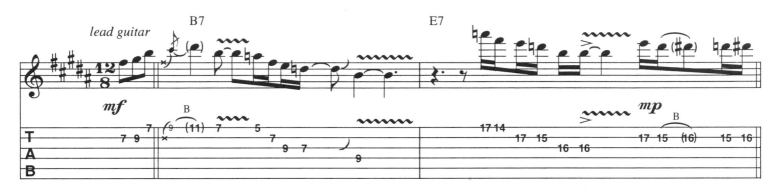

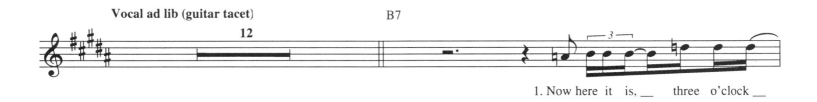

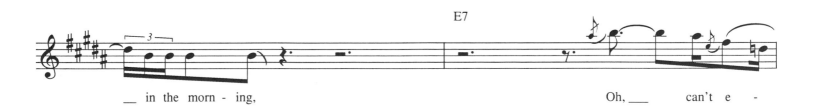

44

4. (Spoken:) A guy feels lone - ly then, when you hear some-thing like that.

You can't do what-ev-er you wan-na do,

hold bend

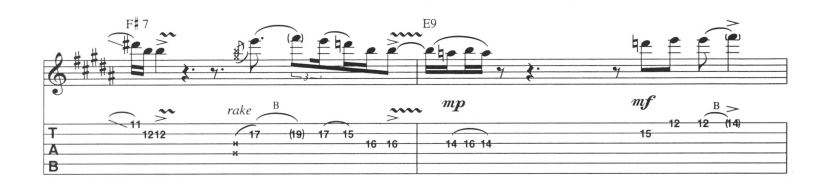

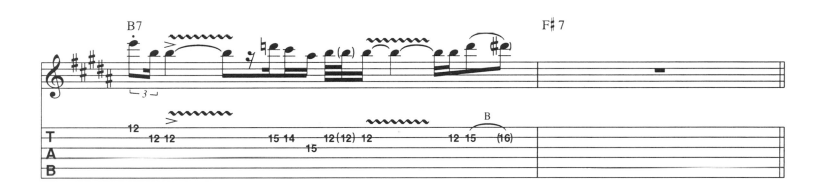

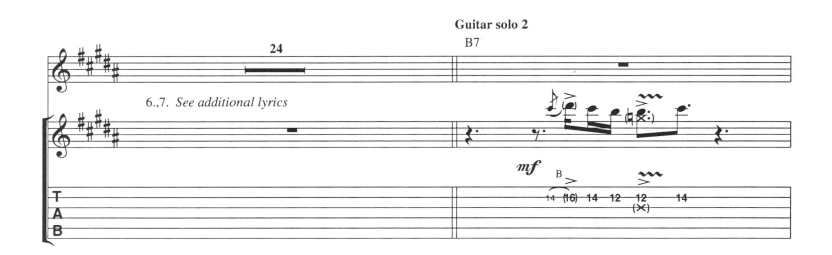

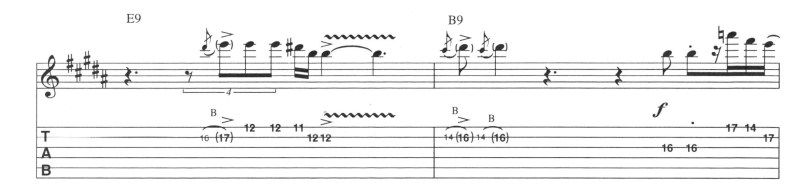

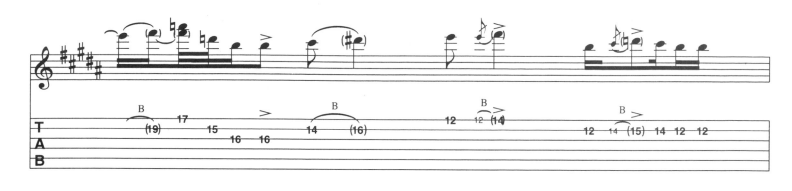

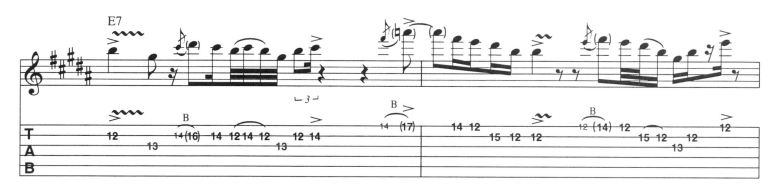

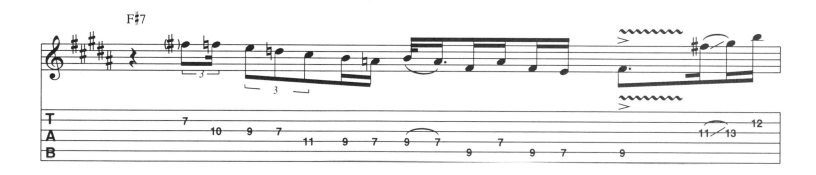

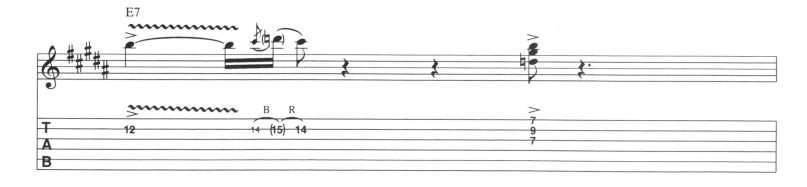

Cadenza
Freely

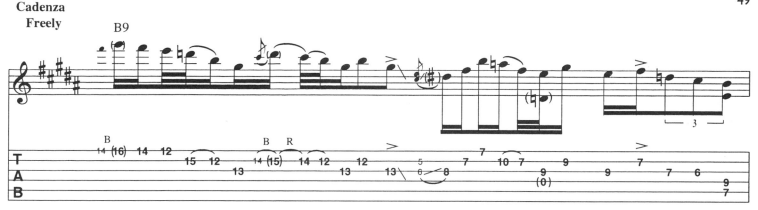

Additional lyrics

2. I've looked around me, people,
   Hey, and my baby she knows she can't be found,
   Looked all around me, people,
   Oh, my baby, she can't be found.
   Well, you know if I don't find my baby,
   People, I'm goin' down to the Golden Ground.
   That's where the fellows hang out down there,
   They shoot pool, you know?

3. Goodbye, everybody,
   Oh, I do believe this is the end,
   Oh, oh, goodbye, everybody,
   Oh, I do believe that this is the end.
   Oh, I want you to tell my baby,
   Oh, to forgive me for my sins.

5. It's my own fault, baby,
   Treat me the way you wanna do,
   Oh, yes, my own fault, baby,
   Treat me the way you wanna do.
   Because when you would love me, baby,
   Oh, a good time looked down,
   That wouldn't be true.

6. I go up on my feet an' I had a lot of friends,
   Now bad luck has hit me people,
   And now I'm down again.
   Oh, I wonder why?
   Why does everything happen to me?
   I'm blue an' I'm lonesome, people,
   My heart is filled with misery.

7. Once I had a lotta money,
   They say the greatest man until,
   But bad luck has hit me now,
   Pain has got me down.
   Yes, I wonder why, people,
   Why does everything have to happen to me?
   I say I'm blue an' I'm lonesome, people,
   My heart is filled with misery.

from Live At The Regal *MCA 27006*

Please Love Me

by B.B. King & Jules Taub

Fast shuffle

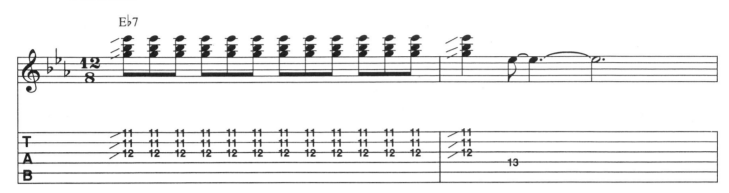

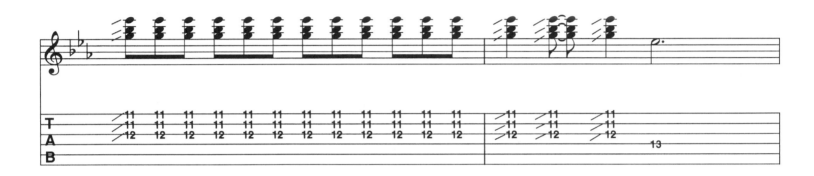

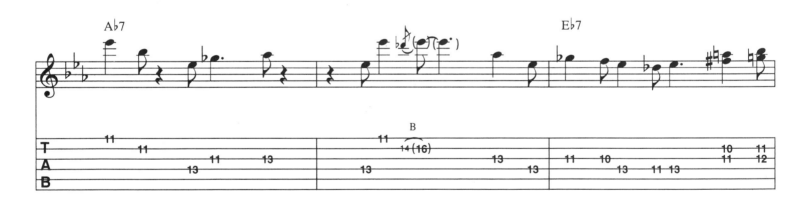

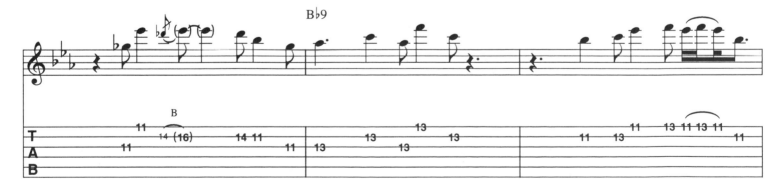

1. I was in love with you,_ ba -

2., 3., 4., 5. *See additional lyrics*

55

Coda

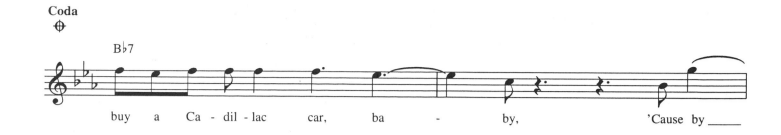

buy a Ca - dil - lac car, ba - by, 'Cause by ____

____ me for - ev - er you are. _____

Additional lyrics

2. You know I love you, baby,
   Do anything you tell me to,
   You know I love you, baby,
   Do anything you tell me to.
   Nothing in this world, baby,
   Honey, that I wouldn't do for you.

3., 4. So if you love me, babe,
   Honey, do everything I say,
   Yes, if you love me, baby,
   Honey do everything I say.
   If you don't do what I tell you, baby,
   Better fall on your knees and pray.

5. Hey, be my girlfriend, (everybody)
   And I'm gonna be your boy,
   Want you to be my girlfriend, baby,
   Baby, I'm gonna be your boy.
   Gonna buy me a Cadillac car, baby,
   'Cause by me forever you are.

from The Electric B.B. King *MCA 27007*

All Over Again

by B.B. King & Jules Taub

That I _____ would be be - ter off _____ dead. ____

Guitar solo

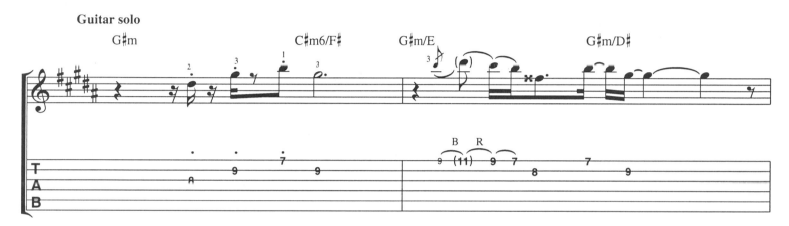

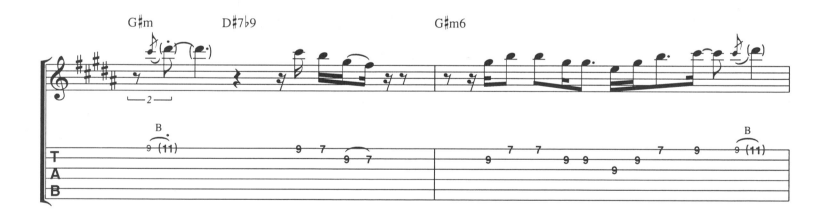

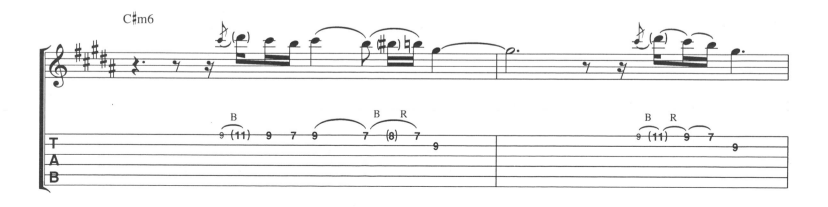

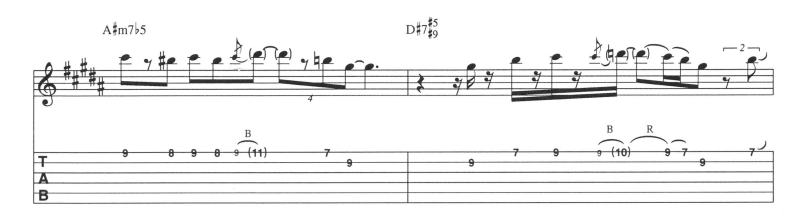

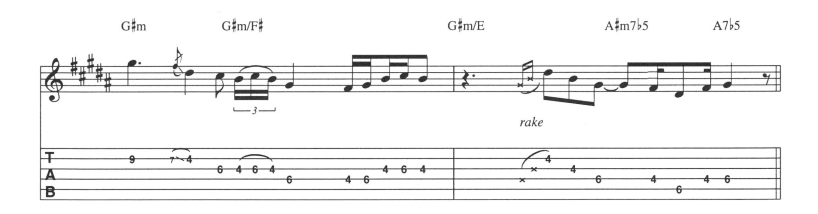

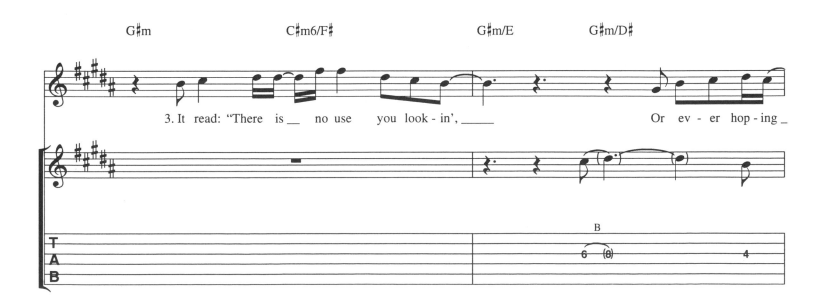

3. It read: "There is __ no use __ you look - in', _____   Or ev - er hop - ing _

from Live "Now Appearing" At Ole Miss MCA 8016

Rock Me Baby
by B.B. King & Joe Josea

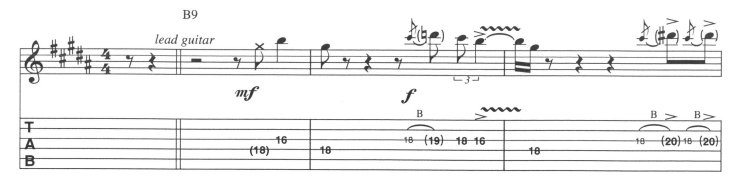

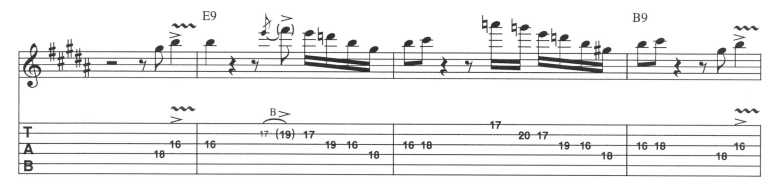

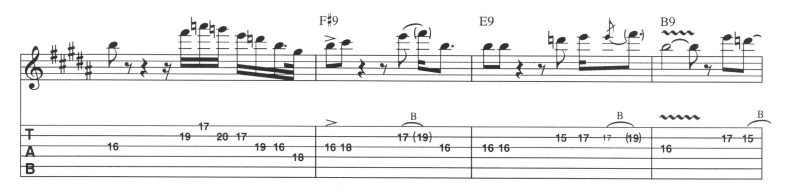

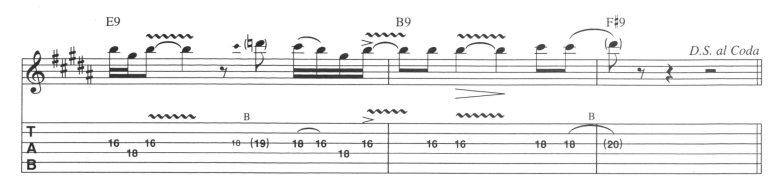

Coda

Guitar solo 2

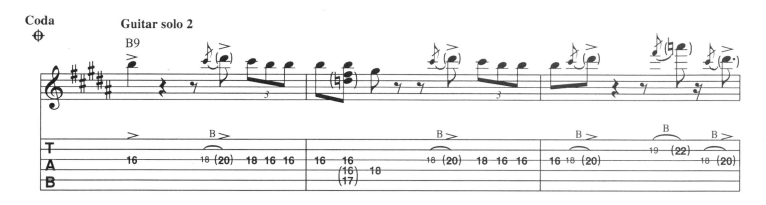

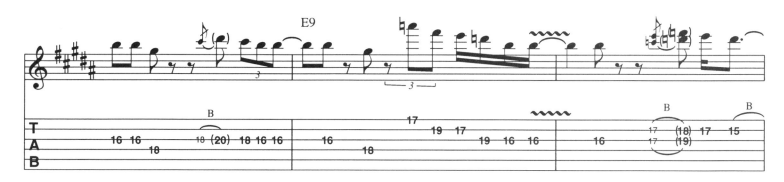

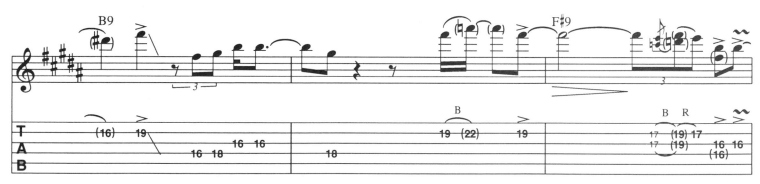

Cadenza
Freely

Additional lyrics

2. Rock me, baby,
   Honey, rock me slow,
   Rock me, baby,
   Honey, rock me slow.
   Rock me, baby,
   'Til I want no more. No!

3. Rock me! (8x)
   Rock me, babe, rock me,
   Rock me all night long,
   One more time.

4. Rock me, go ahead an' say it.
   I can't hear you!
   Rock me! (5x)
   Rock me all night long,
   One more time.

5. Rock me! (12x)

from *Live At The Apollo GRP 9637*

Ain't Nobody's Business

Words and Music by Porter Grainger and Everett Robbins

Ain't no-bod-y's biz-ness what I do. If one day _ I have ham and

ba-con, And the next day _____ ain't noth-in' shak-in', __ No, __ it

ain't, ain't no-bod-y's biz-ness __ what I ____ do.

Guitar solo

from Live At The Apollo *GRP 9637*

Night Life
by Willie Nelson

74

from Live "Now Appearing" At Ole Miss *MCA 8016*

Darlin' You Know I Love You

by B.B. King & Jules Taub

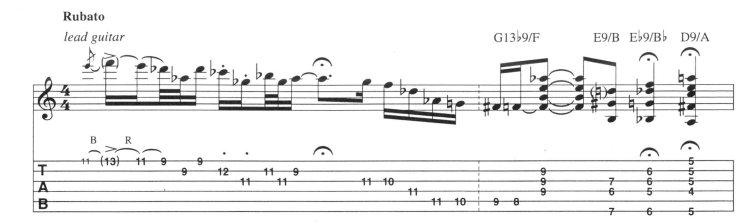

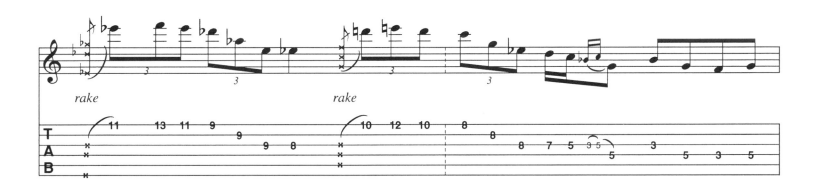

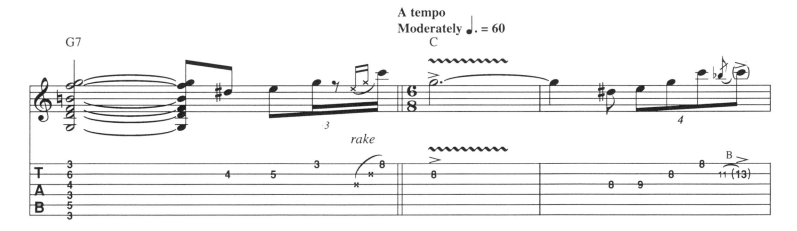

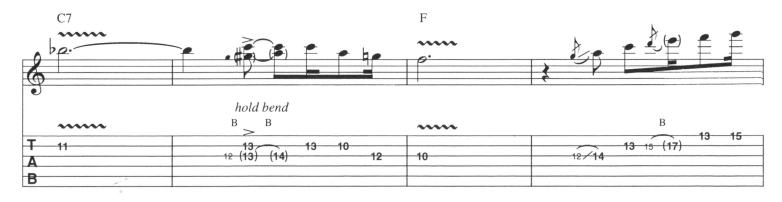

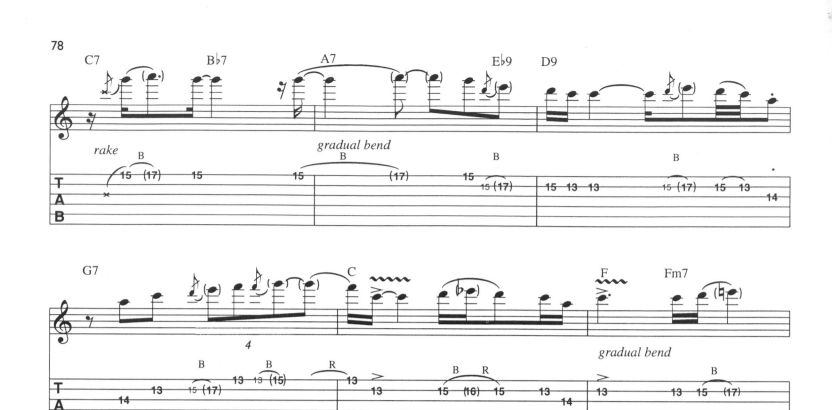

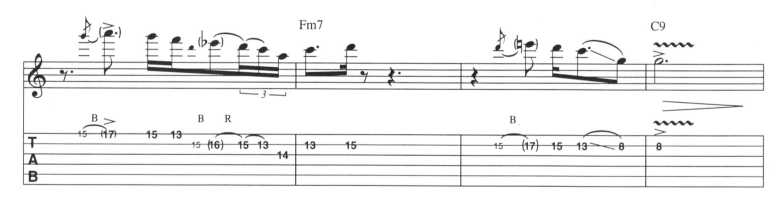

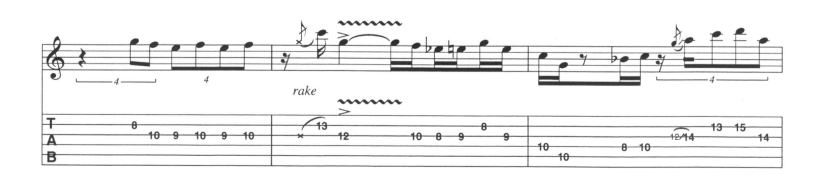

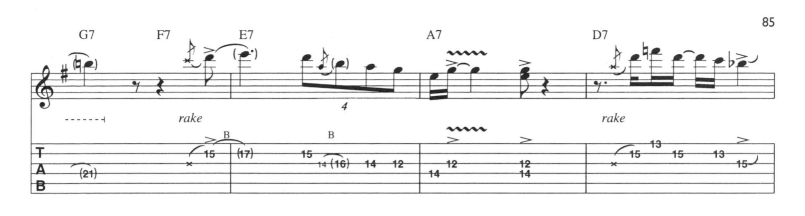

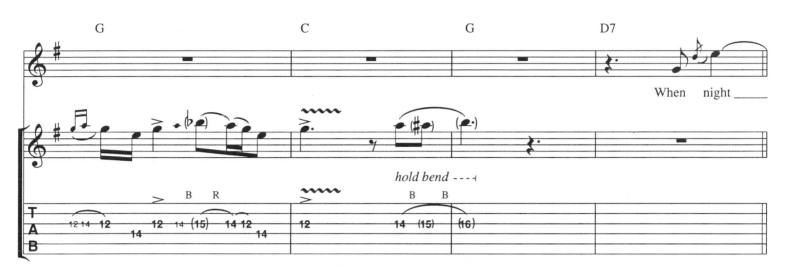

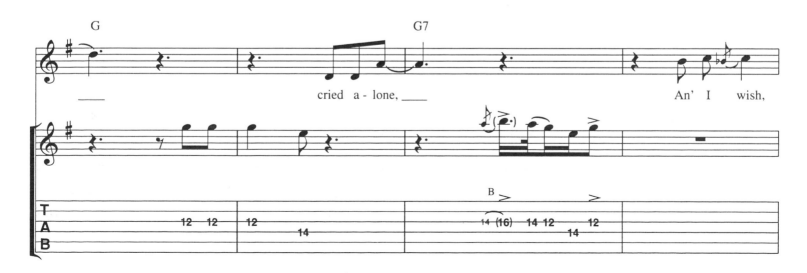

from *Live At The Regal* MCA 27006

You Done Lost Your Good Thing Now

by B.B. King & Joe Josea

Additional lyrics

4. Oh, but let me,
   Let me love you one more time, baby,
   Let me love you one more time, anyway.
   Oh baby,
   Let me love you one more time, anyway.
   Well, you know you can't quit me now, baby,
   Because you didn't mean me no good, anyway.

5. Hey, yeah, baby,
   Baby, you done lost your good thing now,
   Whoa, baby,
   You done lost your good thing now.
   Yes, I'll say the way I used to,
   The way I used to love you, baby,
   Baby, that's the way I hate you now.

from Bobby Bland & B.B. King: Together Again... Live MCA 27012

Let The Good Times Roll

Words and Music by Sam Thread and Fleecie Moore

Moderate blues shuffle (♩♩ = ⌜³⌝♩♪) ♩ = 126

Introduction

lead guitar

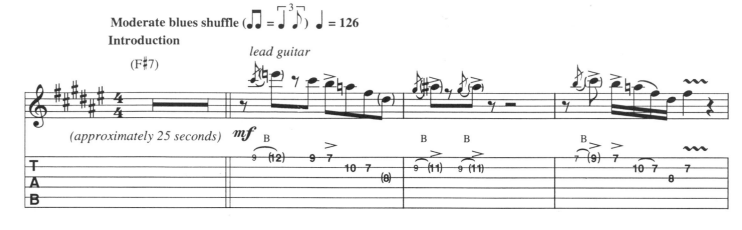

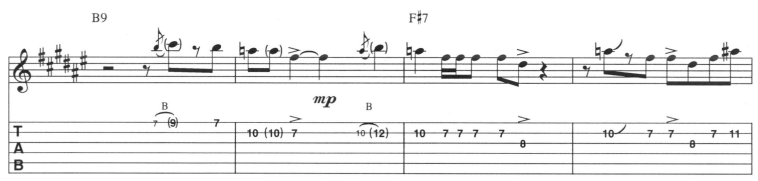

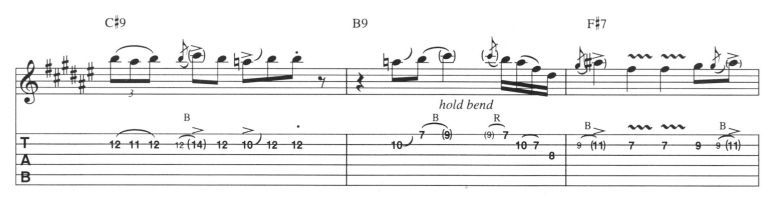

1. Hey, ___ ev'-ry-bod-y,   let's have some _ fun,   You

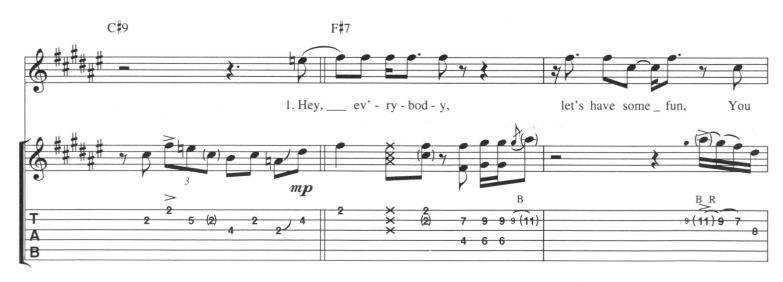

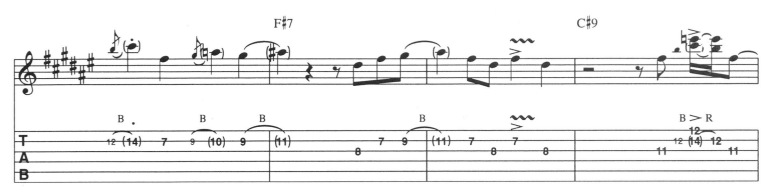

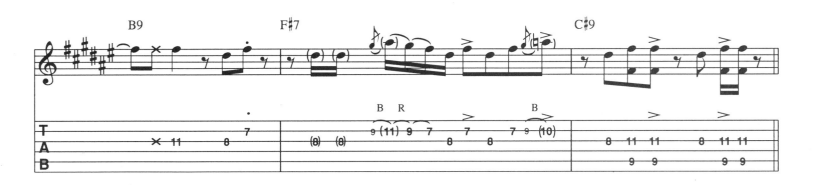

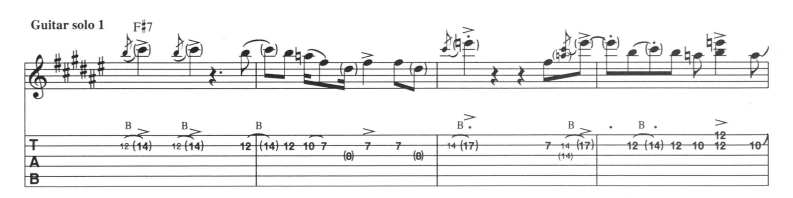

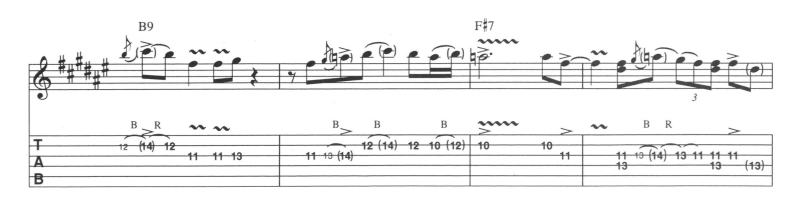

Verse 3 *(See additional lyrics)*

Verse 4 *(See additional lyrics)*

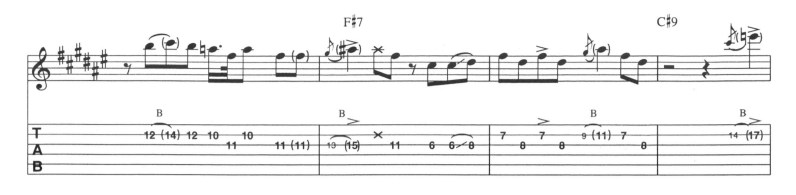

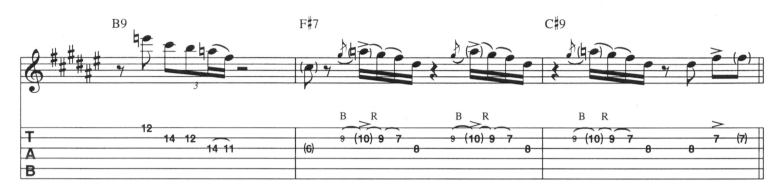

Verse 5 *(See additional lyrics)*

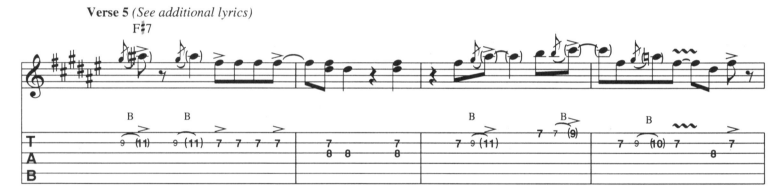

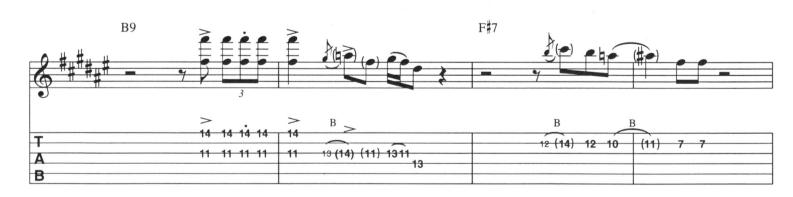

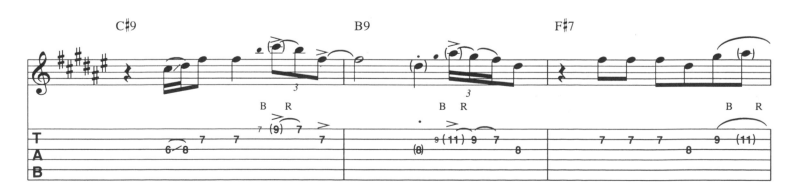

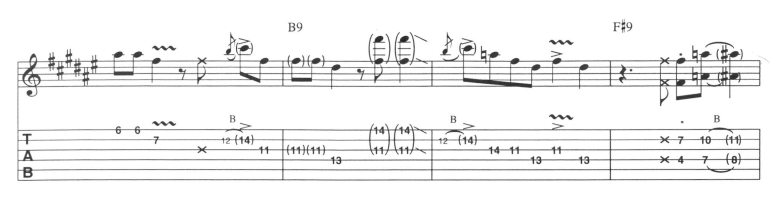

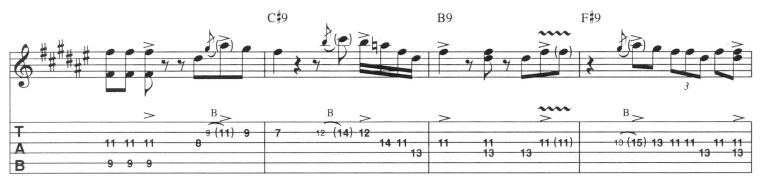

Verse 8 *(See additional lyrics)*

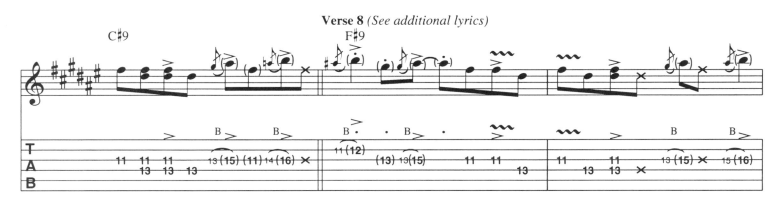

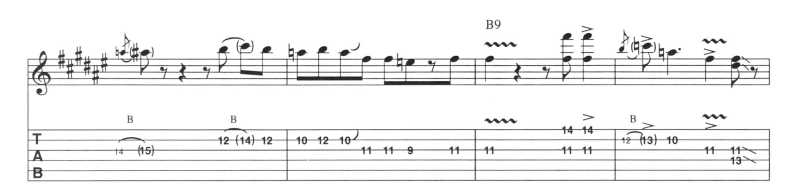

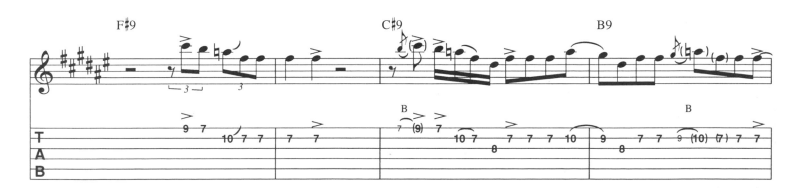

Verse 9 *(See additional lyrics)*

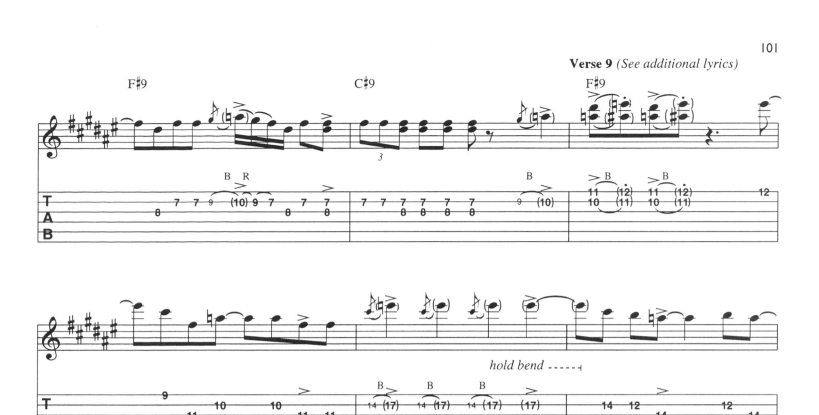

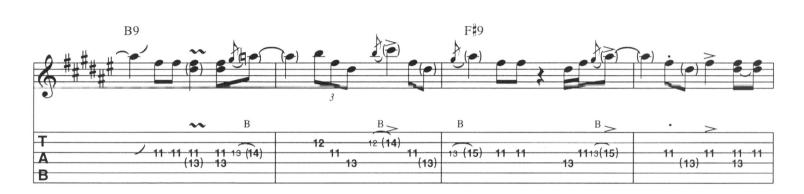

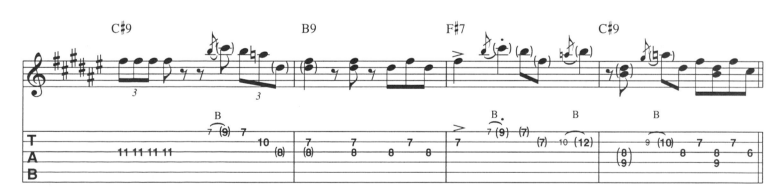

Verse 10 *(See additional lyrics)*

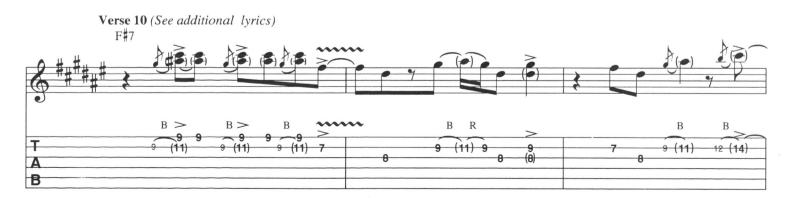

Cadenza
Freely

F#9

(on cue)

Additional lyrics

2. Don't stand there moanin', talkin' trash,
   If you wanna have some fun,
   You better go out an' spend some cash.
   And let the good times roll,
   Let the good times roll.
   I don't care if you young or old,
   Get together an' let the good times roll.
   Look out, son!

3. Don't sit down mumblin', talkin' trash,
   If you wanna have a ball,
   You better spend some cash.
   An' let the good times roll,
   Let the good times roll.
   Heh, I don't care if you young or old,
   That's good enough to let the good times roll.

4. Hey, mister landlord, lock up all the doors,
   When the police comes around,
   Tell them Johnny's comin' down.
   Let the good times roll,
   Let the good times roll.
   An' Lord, I don't care if you young or old,
   That's good enough to let the good times roll.

5. Let 'em roll.
   I don't care if you're young or old,
   Let the good times roll.

6. Hey, ev'-'rybody, tell ev'-'rybody that B.B. 'n Bobby's in town!
   I got a dollar 'n'a quarter,
   An' I'm just rarin' to clown.
   Don't let nobody play me cheap,
   I got fifty cents to know that I'm gonna keep.
   Let the good times roll,
   I don't care if you young or old,
   Let's get together an' let the good times roll.
   Are you ready?

7.-10. Let em' roll!
        Let em' roll!
        Let 'em roll!
        Let 'em roll!

from Live At The Regal *MCA 27006*

Woke Up This Morning

by B.B. King & Jules Taub

Copyright © 1951 by POWERFORCE MUSIC & SOUNDS OF LUCILLE
International Copyright Secured. All Rights Reserved. Used by Permission.

2. I ain't got __ no -   3. Hey _ babe, _____   All __ a - lone _

4.,5. See additional lyrics

__   Yeah, _____ babe, ___   I'm __ all __ a-

lone. __   I ain't had __ no _____ lov - in',   My ba - by been

gone. _____   4. Hey ____ babe, _

Additional lyrics

2. I ain't got nobody,
   Stayin' home with me,
   Aint' got nobody,
   Stayin' home with me.
   My baby, she's gone,
   I'm in misery.

4. Hey babe,
   I'm all alone,
   Oh, babe,
   I'm all alone.
   I ain't had no lovin',
   My baby been gone (everybody).

5. Hey babe,
   I'm all alone,
   Oh, babe,
   I'm all alone.
   I ain't had no lovin',
   My baby been gone.

from The Electric B.B. King *MCA 27007*

Don't Answer The Door

by Jim Johnson

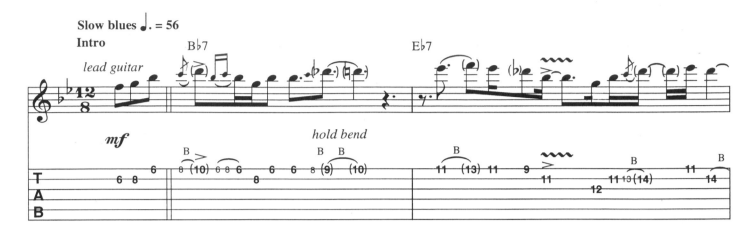

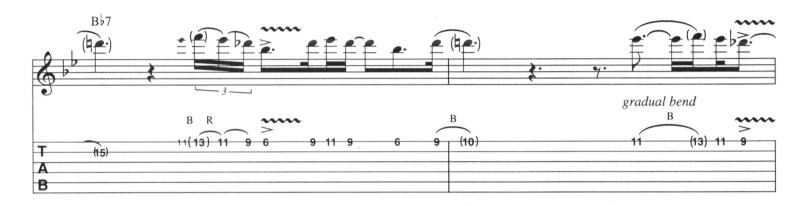

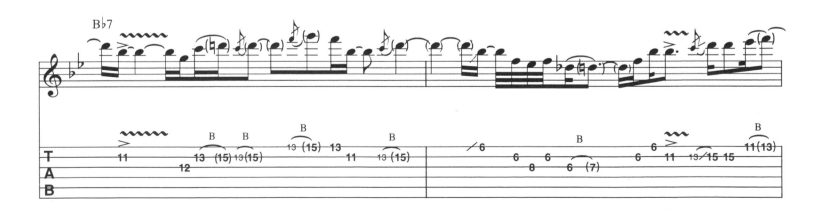

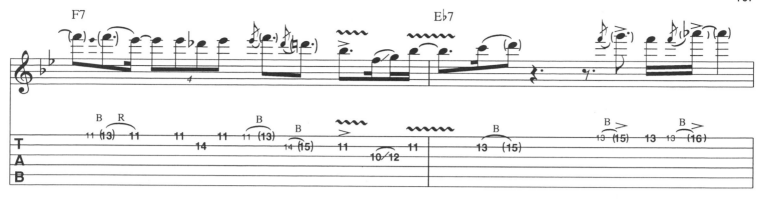

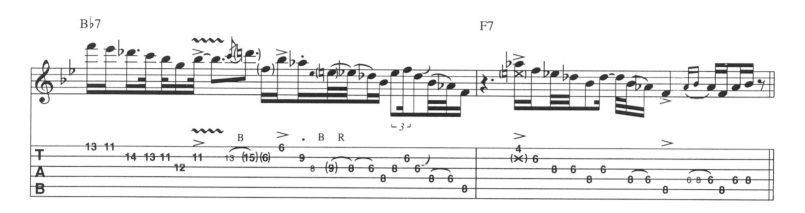

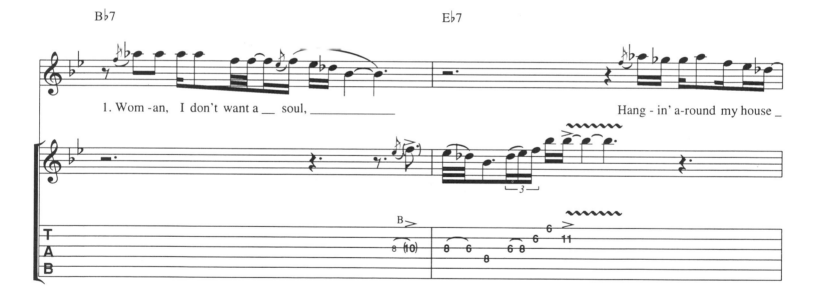

1. Wom-an, I don't want a __ soul, _____ Hang-in' a-round my house __

__ when I'm not __ at home, __ Oh, _____

you to an- swer the door for no-bod-y, ba - by, __

Oh, ____ when you're _ home ____

an' you know you're all __ a - lone. _____

from The Best of B.B. King MCA 27074

Sweet Sixteen

by B.B. King & Joe Josea

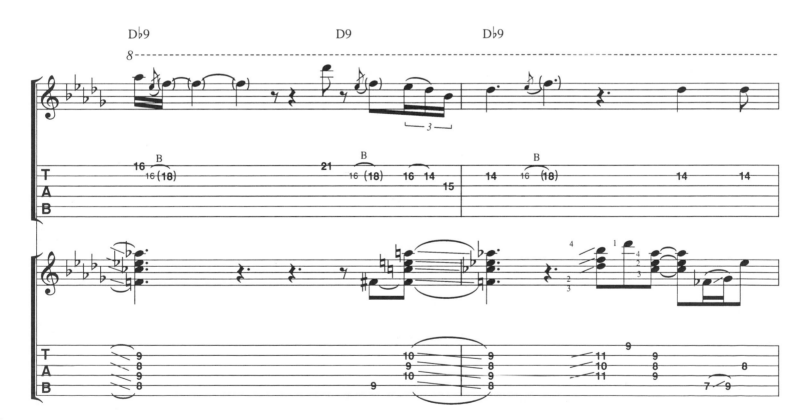

123

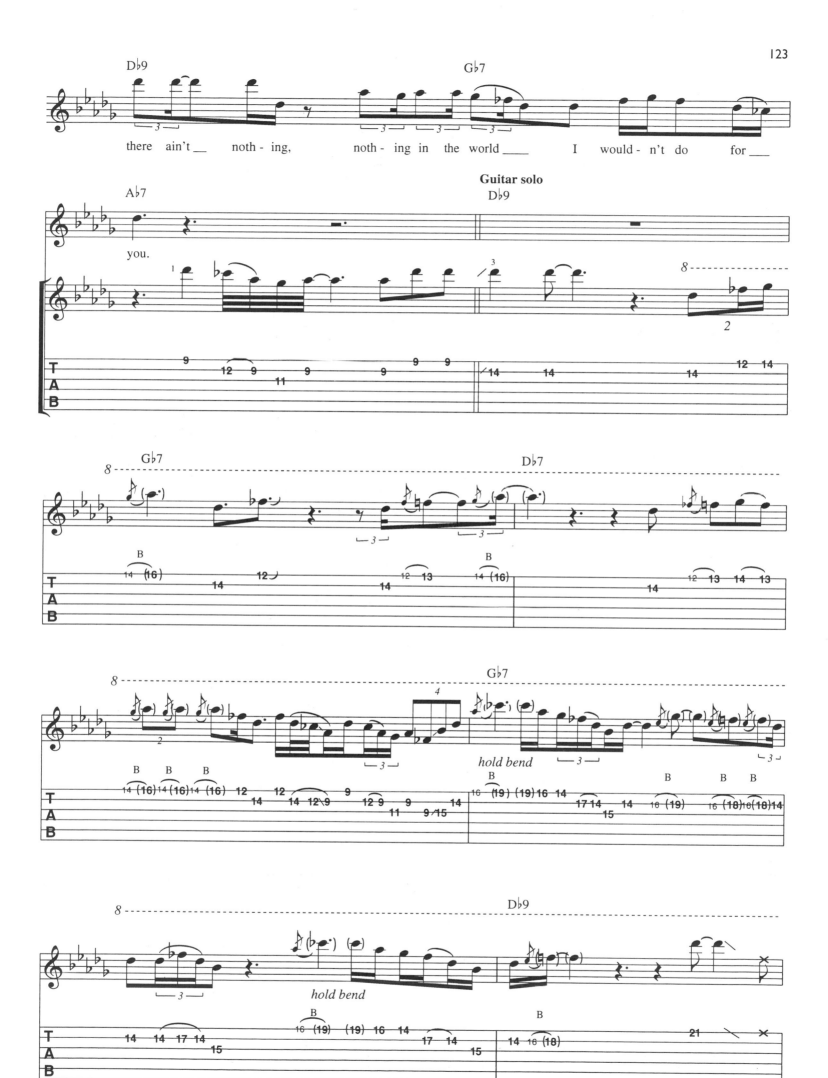

124

from Live At The Regal MCA 27006

You Upset Me Baby
by B.B. King & Jules Taub

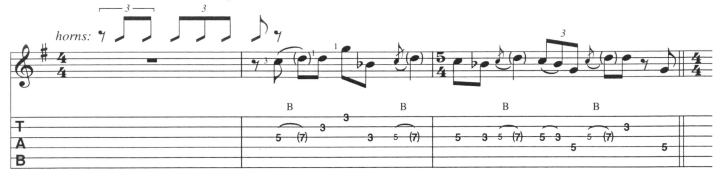

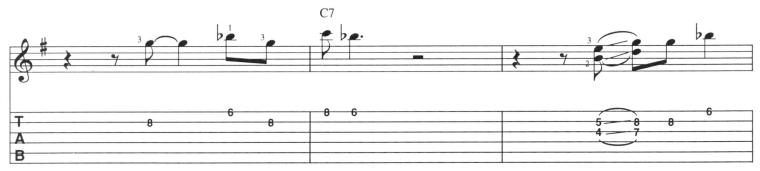

134

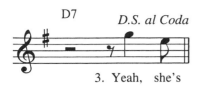

D7   *D.S. al Coda*

3. Yeah, she's

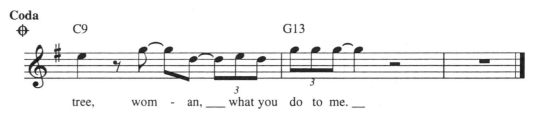

Coda   C9   G13

tree,   wom - an, ___ what you do to me. __

Additional lyrics

2.,3.   Yeah, she's not too tall,
        Complexion is fair,
        Man, she knock me out,
        The way she wear her hair.
        You upset me, baby,
        Yes, you upset me, baby,
        Well, like bein' hit by a fallin' tree,
        Woman, what you do to me, yeah!

4.   Well now, its hard to describe her,
        It's hard to start,
        Better stop now,
        Because I've got a weak heart.
        You upset me, baby,
        Yes, you upset me, baby,
        Well, like bein' hit by a fallin' tree,
        Woman, what you do to me.

from The Best of B.B. King MCA 27074

Why I Sing The Blues
By B.B. King and Dave Clark

1. Ev-'ry-bod-y want to know,   Why I sing the blues, ___   Yes, I
2., 3., 5. - 11. See additional lyrics

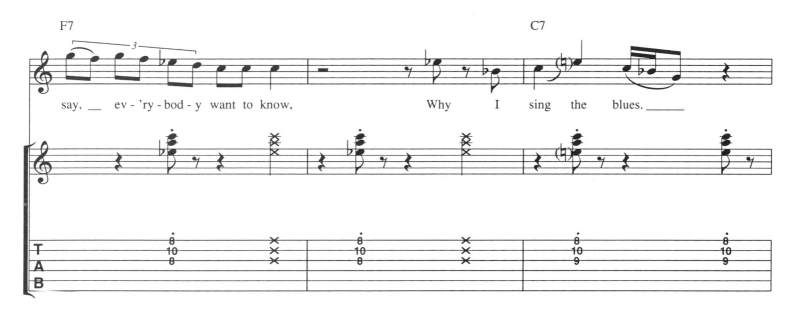

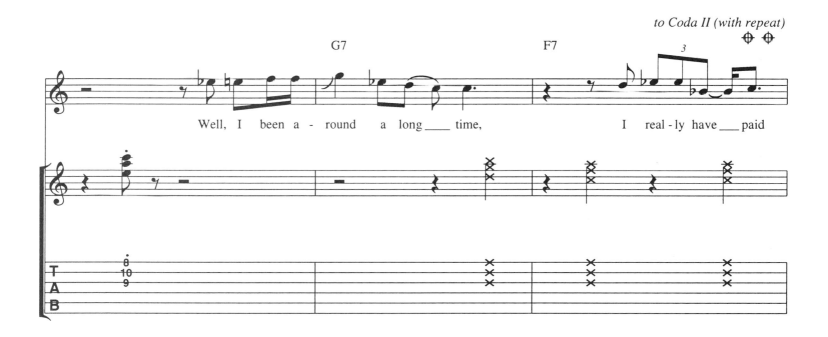

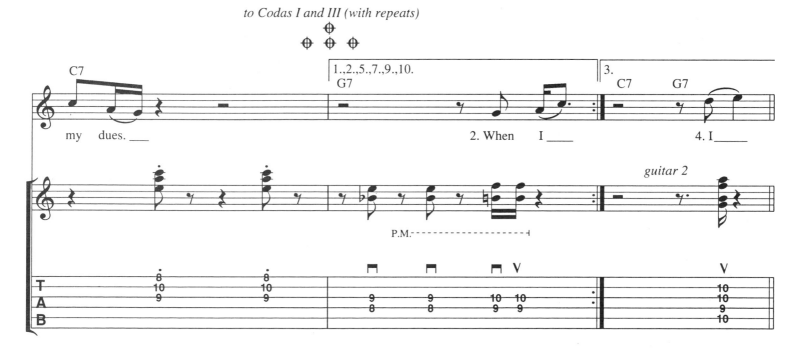

stood __ in line, Down at the coun - ty hall, ___ I heard a man say, "We're gon-na build, _

(guitar 1 continues simile)

___ some new a-part-ments for y'all." _ And ev-'ry-bod-y wan-na know, _____ Yes, they wan-na know why I'm sing-

in' the blues, ___ Yes, I've been a - round a long, long ___ time,

Yes, I've real-ly, real-ly paid ___ my dues. *(Spoken:) "Now I'm gonna play Lucille."*

Guitar solo 1

guitar 2 continues simile

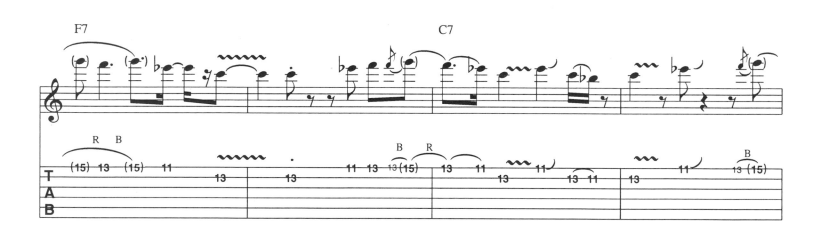

D.S. al Coda I

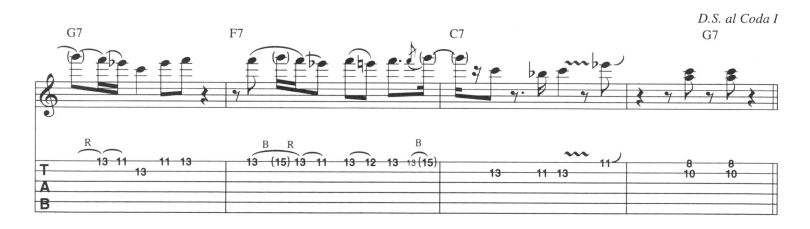

9. Yeah,   they

Coda III

(Spoken:) *"Build it one more time."*

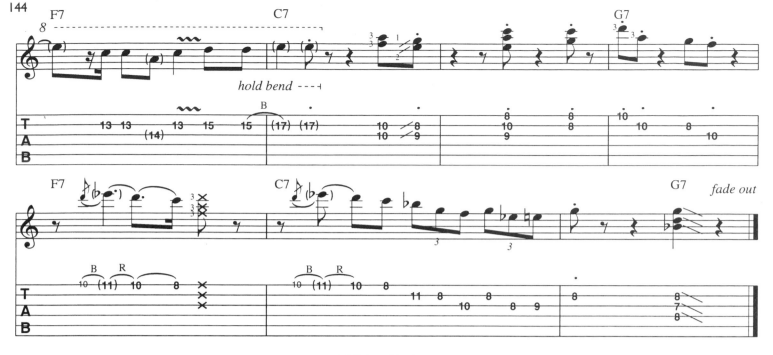

Additional lyrics

2. When I first got the blues,
   They brought me over on a ship,
   Men were standin' over me,
   And a lot more with a whip.
   And everybody wanna know,
   Why I sing the blues,
   Well, I been around a long time,
   Mmmm, I've really paid my dues.

3. I've laid in the ghetto flats,
   Cold and numb,
   I heard the rats tell the bedbugs,
   To give the roaches some.
   Everybody wanna know,
   Why I'm singing the blues,
   Yes, I've been around a long time,
   People, I've paid my dues.

5. My kid's gonna grow up,
   Gonna grow up to be a fool,
   'Cause they ain't got no more room,
   No more room for him in school.
   And everybody wanna know,
   Everybody wanna know why I'm singin' the blues,
   I say I've been around a long time,
   Yes, I've really paid some dues.

6. Yeah, you know the papa, he told me,
   Yes, you're born to lose,
   Everybody around me, people,
   It seems like everybody got the blues.
   But I had 'em a long time,
   I've really, really paid my dues,
   You know, I ain't ashamed of it, people,
   I just love to sing my blues.

7. I walked through the city, people,
   On my bare feet,
   I had a fill of catfish and chitlins,
   Up and down Beale Street.
   You know, I'm singin' the blues,
   Yes, I really, I just have to sing my blues,
   I've been around a long time,
   People, I've really, really paid my dues.

8. Now, father time is catching up with me,
   Gone is my youth,
   I look in the mirror every day,
   And Lordy, tell me the truth.
   I'm singin' the blues,
   Mmmm, I just have to sing the blues,
   I've been around a long time,
   Yes, yes, I've really paid some dues.

9. Yeah, they told me everything would be better for country,
   Mmmm, everything was fine,
   I caught me a bus uptown, baby,
   And every people, all the people
   Got the same trouble as mine.
   I got the blues, aha,
   I say, I've been around a long time,
   Mmmm, I've really paid some dues.
   (One more time, fellas.)

10. Blind man on the corner,
    Beggin' for a dime,
    The rollers come and caught him,
    And throw him in the jail for a crime.
    I got the blues,
    Mmmm, I'm singin' my blues,
    I've been around a long time,
    Mmmm, I've really paid some dues.
    (Can we do just one more?)

11. Oh, I thought I'd go down to the Welfare,
    To get myself some grits and stuff,
    But a lady stood up and she said,
    You haven't been around long enough.
    That's why I got the blues,
    Mmmm, the blues,
    I say I've been around a long time,
    I've really, really paid my dues.
    (Build it one more time.)